TONY ROBINSON'S
WEIRD WORLD OF WONDERS
FUNNY INVENTIONS

Tony Robinson has been scribbling away since he was old enough to pick up a pencil. He's written long stuff (last year he wrote a history of Australia), and shorter stuff (like this). He's rewritten old stories (like the ones about the Greek heroes Odysseus and Theseus), and made up new ones (for instance his children's TV series *Tales from Fat Tulip's Garden*). But history is what he likes best because, he says, 'How do you know who you are if you don't know where you came from?' That's why he's written *Tony Robinson's Weird World of Wonders*, and he doesn't want to stop until he's written about about every single bit of history there's ever been – although in order to do this he'll have to live till he's 8,374!

Del Thorpe has been drawing ever since that time he ruined his mum's best tablecloth with wax crayons. Most of his formative work can be found in the margins of his old school exercise books. His maths teacher described these misunderstood works as 'wasting time'. When he left normal school, Del went to art school and drew serious, grown-up things. Soon he decided the grown-up stuff was mostly boring, so went back to drawing silly cartoons and has done ever since.

Other books by Tony Robinson

The Worst Children's Jobs in History

Bad Kids

Tony Robinson's Weird World of Wonders: Egyptians

Tony Robinson's Weird World of Wonders: Romans

Tony Robinson's Weird World of Wonders: British

Tony Robinson's Weird World of Wonders: Greeks

This book has been specially written and published for World Book Day 2013. For further information, visit www.worldbookday.com

World Book Day in the UK and Ireland is made possible by generous sponsorship from National Book Tokens, participating publishers, authors and booksellers.

Booksellers who accept the £1 World Book Day Book Token bear the full cost of redeeming it.

World Book Day, World Book Night and Quick Reads are annual initiatives designed to encourage everyone in the UK and Ireland – whatever your age – to read more and discover the joy of books.

World Book Night is a celebration of books and reading for adults and teens on 23 April, which sees book gifting and celebrations in thousands of communities around the country: www.worldbooknight.org

Quick Reads provides brilliant short new books by bestselling authors to engage adults in reading: www.quickreads.org.uk

TONY ROBINSON'S
WEIRD WORLD OF WONDERS
funny INVENTIONS

Illustrated by
Del Thorpe

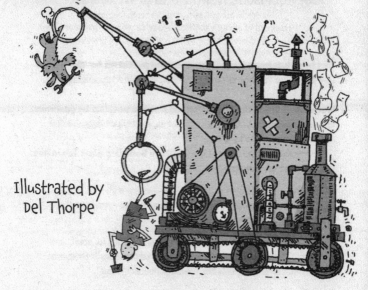

MACMILLAN CHILDREN'S BOOKS

First published 2013 by Macmillan Children's Books
a division of Macmillan Publishers Limited
20 New Wharf Road, London N1 9RR
Basingstoke and Oxford
Associated companies throughout the world
www.panmacmillan.com

ISBN 978-1-4472-3476-0

1 3 5 7 9 8 6 4 2

A CIP catalogue record for this book is available from
the British Library.

Typeset by Dan Newman/Perfect Bound Ltd
Printed and bound by CPI Group (UK) Ltd, Croydon CRO 4YY

Hi! We're the Curiosity Crew. You'll spot us hanging about in this book checking stuff out.

This book is about inventions, but what are they? They're the taps you fill up the kettle from, they're the kettle, the teabag, the mug, the machine that makes the mug and the machine that makes the machine that makes the mug – in fact, everything you take a look at and think, 'That's a good idea.' That's what this book is all about.

TOP INVENTIONS

Inventors are sometimes a bit odd – a lot of them spend their lives in sheds, tweaking and doodling, blowing things up, forgetting to wash and nibbling their own earwax.

But it's thanks to them that we have all the amazing and incredible things that fill our world – from cars to computers to can openers . . .

... and rockets and paper and marshmallows and medicine and glue and telescopes and flip-flops and satellites and non-stick frying pans and ladders and curly fries ...

Without them, we'd all still be living in caves bashing bits of rock together, jumping up and down to keep warm, and waiting for our next meal to walk by!

... and dog bowls!

THE TIN CAN

Before the tin can was invented, food was difficult to keep fresh (remember – there were no fridges or freezers in those days).

Within a week meat went mouldy, vegetables rotted and fish smelt worse than your granny's underpants!

It was even worse for soldiers and explorers who had to carry all their food with them. It was so bad that in 1795, the great French general Napoleon Bonaparte offered a prize of 12,000 francs to anyone who could invent a way to keep food fresh for longer.

Napoleon Bonaparte

I always keep my pâté in here . . . but my generals complain it smells.

A French chef called Nicholas Appert won the prize when he discovered you could keep food fresh if you sealed it tightly in a glass container and then boiled it.

But glass containers were a bit too breakable. In 1810, brilliant British inventor Peter Durand designed a more robust metal container – the first tin can! And thirty years later, Henry Evans invented a machine that could produce sixty tin cans an hour – soon people were using tin cans to store everything from oysters to Spaghetti Bolognese.

Did you know: The famous explorer Sir John Franklin and his team took 8,000 tins of food with them on their expedition to the Arctic in 1845 (just imagine having to eat tinned food for three years!). Unfortunately one of the things used to make their cans was lead, and that's poisonous. They never made it back from the Arctic!

One of the oldest tinned cans of food was a tin of roast veal dated 1823, opened by scientists over 130 years later. There's no record of whether anyone had the guts to eat it!

Getting the food out again was more difficult – you had to use a hammer and chisel until the first tin opener was invented!

11

THE BALLPOINT PEN

Writing in ink used be really messy – you had to dip a pointy stick into a big bottle of ink and then drip it over a bit of paper (getting it all over your fingers and clothes in the process). All the splodges and smudges made it pretty difficult to read.

In the 1930s Laszlo Biro – a Hungarian artist and journalist – got so fed up, he and his brother George decided to invent a totally new type of pen!

The pen they created had a container of quick-drying ink inside it and a tiny metal ball at the end – when the pen moved along the paper, the ball rotated and ink would slowly flow out on to the paper.

It was a revolution in writing!

The Biro brothers opened a factory and started to sell their new 'Biros', or 'ballpoint pens' as we know them today!

Did you know a ballpoint pen can produce up to two miles of writing before the ink runs out?

I'll take your word for it – I've done five metres, and I'm bored, and I've got cramp in my arm.

THE STEAM HORSE

Perhaps the greatest invention ever to come out of Great Britain was the steam engine.

OK . . . so it doesn't sound like the most exciting thing ever invented. An engine that makes steam? I get buckets of steam every time a run a bath and nobody ever called me a genius.

Steam engines are pretty complicated things involving tubes and wheels and lots of hissing and smoking.

Basically they boil up lots of water to produce steam and then the steam is used to drive pumps or rotate wheels.

But the steam produced by steam engines could be used to power all sorts of machines, making them work faster and harder than ever before. Steam engines were put into factories, mills and mines all around Britain so that they could produce more and more stuff like iron, steel and coal.

Soon Britain had iron, steel and coal coming out of its ears – so the Brits started shipping it all round the world and sold it for huge amounts of money. The steam engine made Britain rich.

And then some clever-clogs decided to put an engine on wheels . . .

HOW TO INVENT A STEAM ENGINE

The brainbox who did this was a Cornishman called Richard Trevithick. When he was a boy no one would have guessed that one day he'd do something brilliant. His teachers thought he wasn't very bright – one even said he was disobedient, slow, obstinate and inattentive! But much to everyone's surprise, he grew up to be an engineering whizz (so if you've ever had a bad school report, rest easy – you're probably a genius in-waiting).

Richard's dad had run a mine and whenever he'd had some free time, young Richard tinkered with the engines, making them work better and seeing what new things he could make them do.

You can just imagine it, can't you – there he was, hanging around the mine, nothing to do, watching a steam engine chugging away . . .

Hmm! I wonder what'll happen if I fix this engine upside down on the roof.

17

And ta-da! The steam train was born (or the 'steam horse' as it was originally known).

HORSE

STEAM HORSE

Trevithick showed people his first working railway steam engine (which he called a 'locomotive') in 1804. It was designed to carry iron and coal from the mines and it was incredibly slow, taking four hours to travel just nine miles!

We know who invented the steam engine, but we've got no idea who invented its wheels.

Wheels have been around a *very* long time. The oldest example of a wooden wheel to be found was dug up in Slovenia and it was over 5,000 years old!

A WHEELY GOOD IDEA

The Egyptians only realized how useful wheels could be when an enemy used horse-drawn chariots in an invasion – the first Egyptian to see one in action must have been gobsmacked. But not for long! Within seconds

Love your wheels!

he'd have been running for the nearest shelter ducking the arrows whizzing past his head.

At a stroke battles had become faster and more sudden. Groups of charging chariots carrying archers could break through enemy lines, surround the enemy troops and chase down anyone trying to run away.

The chariot was the sports car of the ancient world. Pharaohs used them as status symbols as well as in battle. When King Tut died, six chariots were buried in his tomb – including a gold one . . . How cool is that? – a bit like being buried with five Ferraris and a golden Range Rover!

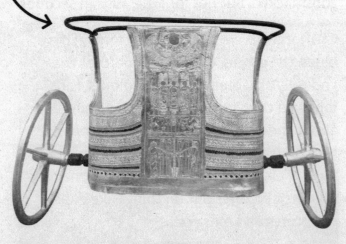

CHARIOT RACING

Chariot racing was Rome's most popular sport – just like football is today. And the 'Circus Maximus' was Rome's Wembley Stadium. In fact it was bigger! It could hold up to 250,000 people – almost three times the number of people who can fit into Wembley – and entry was free!

Charioteers were divided into teams – the blues, the greens, the whites and the reds – and they all wore their team colours. Fans followed their favourite team and knew all about the different horses and drivers. The best drivers were treated like premiership footballers – they earned loads of money and had their pictures put on things like cups, sculptures and mosaics.

LEONARDO DA VINCI –
INVENTOR EXTRAORDINAIRE

In 1478 the famous Italian inventor Leonardo da Vinci drew up plans for the world's first self-propelled vehicle. It was a three-wheeled cart which worked like a wind-up toy – rotating the wheels backwards wound up springs inside and when it was released the cart flew forward! Unfortunately it never really caught on. (I wonder why!)

Leonardo da Vinci may not have got very far in his car but that didn't stop him. He designed loads of extraordinary machines, gadgets and thingummybobs – including a giant crossbow, a flying machine, an eight-barrelled machine gun, a submarine, a tank, a calculator and a parachute – hundreds of years before anybody else thought of them. He was interested in everything – plants, rocks and the human body – and wanted to find out how it all worked.

Oh . . . AND he also happened to be a first-class artist – painting lots of paintings including the world-famous smiling 'Mona Lisa'. People wonder what she's smiling at – probably one of his crazy machines.

The first real cars didn't appear until the twentieth century and the invention of . . .

THE INTERNAL COMBUSTION ENGINE

Ever looked inside a car to see what makes it work? Lift the bonnet and you'll see a big lump of metal, tubes and wires. This is the 'engine' and it makes the car move. Without one, your family's car would just be a big ugly metal box sat in front of your house.

Combustion means 'burning'. Liquid fuel is burned in thousands of tiny explosions inside the engine, which produce lots of gas really fast, which pushes pistons, which turn a series of wheels – causing the car to move.

German egghead engineer Karl Benz designed the first 'internal combustion engine' in 1885 and fitted it to a three-wheeled wagon. He called it a 'Motorwagen', and when he drove it through the streets all the noise and smoke terrified onlookers!

Where do I go?

Nowhere, mate – I'm a horseless carriage.

I've never liked convertibles . . .

In 1888, Karl's wife Bertha took their two kids on a heroic trip to visit their granny in the Motorwagen to show everybody how safe it was to drive a car. It was certainly safe, and they made the fifty-mile journey to Granny's house, but it wasn't reliable. They broke down a few times and had to push it up a hill!

Certainly not everybody was convinced by Karl's newfangled machine – it wasn't just unreliable, it was weird-looking and expensive. At that time you could buy five horses for the price of a car and still have change for a small scooter!

It wasn't until 1908 that American engineer and businessman Henry Ford started making cars that everyone could own. He built a factory that could make cars really quickly. Each part of it made one bit of the car; that way, they could produce a finished car every fifteen minutes!

You didn't have a lot of choice about the colour – to speed up the process of making the cars, they used a special fast-drying black paint. So Ford's car was available in 'any colour as long as it's black'!

I wish they'd hurry up and invent car heaters!

RUBBER

The first car tyres were made of wood or metal – driving an early car on a bumpy road was a bit like being shaken about in a washing machine.

Today all car tyres are made of an amazing bouncy, tough, waterproof material called rubber. It isn't just car tyres that are made of rubber – elastic bands, wellington boots, bath plugs, basketballs and balloons are all made of . . . you guessed it – rubber!

Rubber was called 'rubber' because it was good at rubbing out pencil marks on paper. Which is why the rubber in your pencil case is made of rubber!

Rubber wasn't invented by scientists – it comes from trees in South America where the local tribes used it to make bouncy balls and waterproof shoes.

When people all over the world heard about rubber, they got excited and started making all sorts of things out of this great new material.

But it turned out there was a small problem with rubber ... In the cold of winter it became solid and cracked, and in the heat of summer it melted into a big, gooey, foul-smelling mess! Unhappy customers returned their rubber goods, and rubber merchants went out of business ... It seemed rubber wasn't all it was cracked up to be.

And that would have been that, if it hadn't been for Charles Goodyear. He was a struggling inventor in America who thought that there had to be a way to make rubber better. He started experimenting – cooking it on his kitchen stove, mixing it with different chemicals, baking it in the oven, steaming it over a kettle and rolling it out with a rolling pin. The result was a right old mess – like a cookery class gone horribly wrong!

Finally in 1892 after more than fifty years of testing (and ruining his lovely kitchen) he found the right rubber recipe. His rubber stayed rubbery all year long, in any temperature!

Sales of rubber goods rocketed and they've been popular ever since!

As for Goodyear – he became a bit obsessed. He wore rubber hats, vests and ties. He had his portrait painted on rubber, the story of his life printed on rubber, and tried to make musical instruments, banknotes and jewellery out of rubber. Rubbertastic!

TRAINERS

Rubber was also used to make the first pair of trainers!

In the nineteenth century seaside holidays became popular, but people didn't want to wear leather boots at the beach – so ingenious inventor John Boyd Dunlop designed a new type of lightweight shoe with rubber soles and cotton tops, called 'sand shoes' – which kept your feet cool in summer and dried quickly after a paddle in the sea. They were the prototype of the modern trainer!

Rubber-soled shoes soon started to be worn to play sports. The rubber soles were given ridges and grooves so they could grip the ground. In 1917, in America, these shoes were given the name 'sneakers' because the rubber sole meant you could 'sneak around' quietly in them. Shhhh!

THE PRINTING PRESS

One inventor I'm particularly grateful to is Johannes Gutenberg – and you should be too! If it wasn't for this German genius, you wouldn't be reading this book . . . or *any* book in fact.

In the fifteenth century, Johannes invented a machine to print books! Before printing, if you wanted to make a book you had to write one by hand.

How long have you been working on this dictionary?

Ten years, and I'm only up to the word 'dog'.

If you wanted more copies to give a few to your mates, you had to write the whole thing out again, and again, and again until your hand fell off.

Writing out a copy of the Bible took about two years!

This meant there were hardly any books about, so they were incredibly expensive!

Johannes designed a way to print whole pages of words on to pieces of paper by making little metal blocks (called 'type') with each letter of the alphabet on.

This is what Gutenberg's press would have looked like.

These were then put together to form words and slid into a wooden frame. When one frame was ready, it was covered in ink and a sheet of paper was pressed down on to it.

This is what pieces of metal type looked like.

Help! I've been typecast!

Gutenberg's press was a huge hit. Books, newspapers, magazines and leaflets could be all be made really quickly and soon everyone was reading them!

Is it a car?

Is it a combine harvester?

No I'm a printing press!

THE CLOCK

The earliest clocks were 'sundials' – basically a stick in the ground, which you could use to measure the time of day by the length of the shadow cast by the sun.

Ancient Egyptians and Romans used sundials to mark the passing of the day and to know when to eat meals or have meetings. The snag was they only worked in the daytime . . . and on sunny days!

What time is it?

Erm . . . night time.

WATER TIME IS IT?

The Greeks invented water clocks. I know water and clocks don't normally go together; if you pour water into a clock, it'll stop!

But the Greeks didn't use the type of clocks we have today. They took a small clay pot and put a little hole in the base. Then they filled it with water. As the water leaked out, the level went down and revealed lines drawn on the inside of the pot, which told you how much time had gone by. Clever, eh?

Water clocks worked at any time of day, but some unlucky person needed to be on hand to keep filling it with water!

I can help fill your clock if you're not fussy about the 'water'!

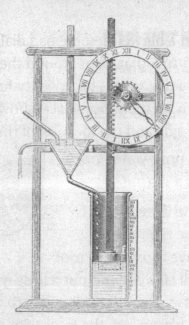

This water clock only had one hand to show the time. At noon someone had to empty the water out.

By the thirteenth century the first mechanical clocks had been invented – these used falling weights to move the cogs and wheels and mark the passing time. They were put in church towers so that everyone knew when to come and pray. Early clocks didn't always have faces. Most people back then couldn't tell the time or read numbers, so they just listened for the bell!

Later clocks were given faces and then hour hands (the minute hand wasn't invented until the seventeenth century!) – but they still looked a bit weird: some had dials numbered from 1 to 6 that went around the clock four times a day, others had twenty-four hours written on them. Some also showed the level of the tide and the location of the planets!

An astronomical clock in Bern, Switzerland.

In 1585 a clockmaker in Germany made a clock mounted on a model ship. It could roll down the middle of a dining table, while a tiny pipe organ played a tune and the masts and sails twirled around until it came to a stop and fired eleven tiny cannon at the dinner guests!

Clocks gradually became smaller and smaller – until they could fit in your pocket. Clock mechanisms became even more complicated and fiddly to design. Early clockmakers were brilliant at design technology – like computer programmers today!

looked a bit weird: some had dials numbered from 1 to 6 that went around the clock four times a day, others had twenty-four hours written on them. Some also showed the level of the tide and the location of the planets!

An astronomical clock in Bern, Switzerland.

In 1585 a clockmaker in Germany made a clock mounted on a model ship. It could roll down the middle of a dining table, while a tiny pipe organ played a tune and the masts and sails twirled around until it came to a stop and fired eleven tiny cannon at the dinner guests!

Did you know: Until the 1920s, men carried their watches on chains in their pockets – wristwatches were thought to be for girls. One gentlemen said he would rather wear a skirt than a wristwatch! This all changed in World War One when it was decided that when you're in the middle of a nasty battle, having a watch attached to your wrist was more sensible than having it waving about on a chain.

Clocks gradually became smaller and smaller – until they could fit in your pocket. Clock mechanisms became even more complicated and fiddly to design. Early clockmakers were brilliant at design technology – like computer programmers today!

The Greeks invented a lot more than just water clocks. Next time somebody asks you what's so great about the Greeks you can wow them with this list of amazing things the geeky Greeks invented . . .

THE FIRST COMPUTER

In 1900, divers found a strange object in an ancient shipwreck under water off the Greek island of Antikythera ('Ant-i-kith-ear-a'). It was a machine about the size of a shoebox made of lots of little rusty metal cogs and gears.

Experts think it was made by the Greeks to calculate the movement of the planets on any given day. Which technically makes it the first computer ever invented!

Cool computer.

Can you play games on it?

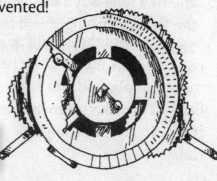

CATAPULTS

Catapults are weapons that fire missiles (arrows, stones or even sometimes cows) at an enemy a long way away. The word comes from the Greek meaning 'shield piercer'. The Greeks designed massively powerful catapults – some which were wound up and then released two missiles at once!

THE ALARM CLOCK

Around 380 BC, the teacher Plato designed a water clock with an alarm to help his students arrive at his lectures on time! It was made of a pot, which slowly filled up with water. When the level of water reached the top, it tipped a bowl of lead balls on to a copper plate and made a ringing sound!

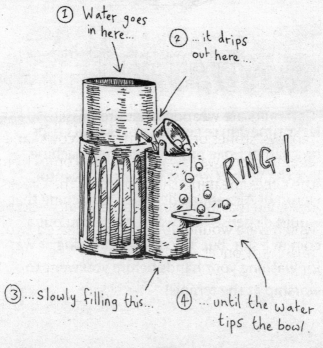

① Water goes in here...

② ...it drips out here...

RING!

③ ...slowly filling this...

④ ...until the water tips the bowl!

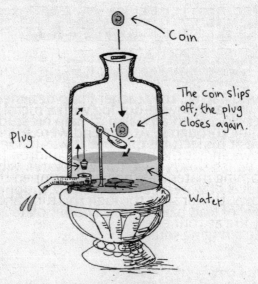

Coin

The coin slips off; the plug closes again.

Plug

Water

THE VENDING MACHINE

Next time you're getting a packet of crisps or a can of Coke out of a vending machine, just thank the Greeks! The Greek inventor Heron of Alexandria designed a machine that would dispense holy water when you put a coin in a slot. But it wasn't for drinking, it was for washing your hands before you went to worship at the temple!

THE FLAME-THROWER

This was a hollowed-out log with a metal pipe running through it. At one end were some bellows and at the other was a cauldron full of flaming material. When you pumped the bellows, the air shot through the tube and blew fire at your enemy!

THE ALPHABET

Did you know that the Greeks came up with lots of the letters we use today? The name 'Alphabet' even comes from the Greek for A and B (Alpha and Beta).

Aα	Bβ	Xχ	Δδ	Eε
Aa	Bb	Cc	Dd	Ee
Φφ	Γγ	Hη	Iι	φϑ
Ff	Gg	Hh	Ii	Jj
Kκ	Λλ	Mμ	Nν	Oo
Kk	Ll	Mm	Nn	Oo
Ππ	Θθ	Pρ	Σσ	Tτ
Pp	Qq	Rr	Ss	Tt
Yυ	ϖς	Ωω	Ξξ	Ψψ
Uu	Vv	Ww	Xx	Yy
Zζ				
Zz				

AUTOMATIC DOORS

Heron of Alexandria also designed temple doors which opened automatically. At the same time trumpets started to play, fog was pumped out and statues and metallic birds started singing ... which must have completely freaked the worshippers out!

SECRET CODES

The Greek historian Polybius came up with a way of sending messages without writing them down. He invented a code which could be sent using fire beacons over long distances – each arrangement of torches signalled a different letter and nobody watching would know what you were saying!

THE DEATH RAY

The Greek mathematician Archimedes was a bit mad. They say he was once sitting in the bath when he had a great idea and was so excited he jumped up and ran through the streets naked shouting 'I've got it!' One of his most bizarre inventions was the 'death ray' – a series of mirrors which concentrated sunlight on to enemy ships and set them on fire!

SHOWERS

And last but not least, the Greeks loved having a good scrub at the public baths and were the first people with showers . . . freezing cold ones!

While we're in the bathroom, it's time to introduce . . .

THE FLUSHING TOILET

The flushing toilet may be over 5,000 years old – experts studying the remains of a Stone Age village on the Orkney Islands in Scotland found that the houses contained little closets with drains underneath that were flushed by the nearby river!

The first *official* flushing toilet was invented in 1585 by Sir John Harrington, as a present to Queen Elizabeth I of England. When you pulled a knob, it emptied water into the toilet and flushed it into a vault under the floor.

Legend has it that the Queen was reluctant to use her new flush because it was too noisy and would alert everybody to the fact she was on the loo! The flushing toilet didn't catch on for another 300 years!

PLEASE DON'T NICK THE STICK

HMMN

Roman toilets could sit up to sixty people – yikes!

THE PUBLIC TOILET

Many Romans didn't have their own loo, but you could pay a small fee to use a public toilet, where you sat on a bench and did your business through a hole into a channel below. It wasn't very private – you just sat between lots of other people doing the same thing, and when you wanted to wipe your bum someone passed you a sponge on a stick . . . which is the origin of our phrase 'getting the wrong end of the stick'. Eewww!

Did you know: Before flushing loos were introduced, boys were employed as 'gong scourers' ('gong' was an old word for toilet) – their job was to clean the sewers and chambers underneath toilets and stop them getting blocked up. They spent hours up to their necks in other people's poo and sometimes passed out from the smell . . . I can't imagine a worse job, can you?

The poo was taken to the edge of town and dumped to be used as fertilizer. Some dumps became massive – one named 'Mount Pleasant' in London covered 7.5 acres by 1780 (that's over four football pitches!).

By 1800, people started to realize that having piles of poo lying around wasn't very hygienic. Horrible diseases like cholera, dysentery and typhus spread and killed lots of people every year.

In 1861, crafty plumber Thomas Crapper started making and selling flushing toilets – he encouraged lots of people to buy one for their homes. From now on human poo would be flushed away down the toilet and into a system of pipes that took it safely out to sea. Good news for the 'gong scourers'! (Not such good news for fish . . .)

The first packaged toilet paper was made in America in 1857, and in 1880 the British Perforated Paper Company created paper that came in boxes of pre-cut squares. Loo rolls didn't become common until 1907.

Early toilet brushes were made of hair from horses, squirrels and badgers!

Who's nicked my tail?

Some of the first public toilets in Britain (or 'monkey closets' as they were known) were installed at the Great Exhibition in 1851. More than 800,000 people paid a penny to use them – which is where the term 'spend a penny' comes from! Unfortunately, once you were inside you had to keep one hand firmly on the door handle, because they didn't have locks. The vacant/engaged bolt wasn't invented until thirty years later!

Crikey, is this the queue for the loo?

THE CHOCOLATE CHIP COOKIE

In 1930 Ruth Wakefield, owner of the Toll House Inn in Massachusetts, America, was making chocolate cookies for her guests one day and tried dropping broken pieces of chocolate into the mix.

Instead of melting to create chocolate-flavour cookies as she expected, she found she'd invented the first chocolate chip cookie! They became really popular and she sold her recipe to a chocolate company in return for a lifetime's supply of chocolate chips!

THE LAST STRAW

Until the nineteenth century straws were made of, well . . . straw!

The problem was that your drink tasted of straw. Which is OK if you're a horse, but not if you're not.

In the 1880s, American inventor Marvin Chester Stone designed the first manmade drinking straw by wrapping a piece of paper round a pencil and gluing it at the ends, then dipping it in wax to make it waterproof.

Did you know: The first evidence of straws comes from an ancient Sumerian tomb – a picture found in the tomb shows two men drinking beer with straws 5,000 years ago!

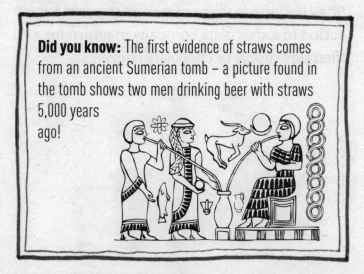

Fifty years later Joseph B. Friedman perfected the design after sitting in an ice-cream parlour and watching his daughter Judith struggle to drink her big milkshake through a straight straw.

He poked a screw down the straw and wound dental floss round it to make creases in the straw. When he took the screw out, he'd created an accordian-like ridge in the once-straight straw! In other words he'd made the first bendy straw!

His first big sale was to a hospital – where nurses realized the bendy straw would help bed-ridden patients reach their drinks!

Nope, I still can't reach.

ELECTRIC DREAMS

Flying a kite in a thunderstorm – what could possibly go wrong?

From the 1750s onwards scientists all over the world were experimenting with electricity. They did lots of crazy stunts like flying kites in storms to try and capture the lightning flashing across the sky.

Of course you and I know that this is really dumb behaviour, because electricity is dangerous and you could end up with sticky-out hair and fried eyeballs. But these nutty scientists found this out the hard way . . .

In 1753, a German called Georg Wilhelm Richmann tried to capture the electricity in a storm cloud by using a long metal rod attached to the roof of his house. He was struck by lightning which killed him stone dead and blew both his shoes off!

Fortunately for scientists everywhere, they finally worked out better ways to generate electricity using chemical reactions and magnets. It wasn't long before electricity was powering a whole new generation of machines!

Did you know: Some of the earliest encounters with electricity were in ancient Egypt when people got shocks from electric fish! Some fish – like the catfish and torpedo ray – give off electric shocks to stop predators eating them. One ancient Roman doctor advised his patients to stand on a live electric fish to cure headaches!

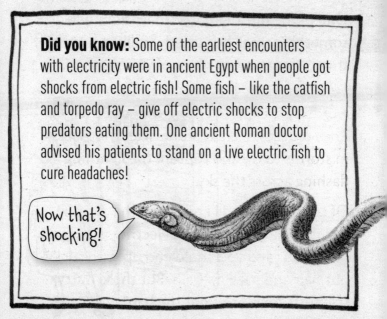

Now that's shocking!

Once electricity had been discovered, scientists and engineers went crazy devising all sorts of new electric-powered devices – electric toasters, electric irons, electric hairdryers, electric ovens, electric fans and electric blankets.

One of the most fantastic inventions was something small but utterly brilliant – today there's one in every room of your house . . .

THE LIGHT BULB

Before electric lighting, people used candles and gas lamps to light their homes. Good candles were expensive so poor people made them out of animal fat – which gave off lots of thick black smoke and smelt like a burning barnyard . . . Blurgh!

In 1800, brainbox English scientist Humphry Davy produced the first electric light. He sent electricity through a stick of charcoal which burned white hot, producing a dazzling bright light. This was OK for outside but it wasn't very good for lighting the home – it was just too bright!

Just imagine getting out of bed, switching on your light and having to put on sunglasses in case your eyeballs burned up!

Scientists began to search for ways to produce a gentler light. American inventor Thomas Edison hit the jackpot in 1879 when he designed the 'light bulb' – which used hardly any electricity, and made a small piece of carbon thread glow gently inside a glass globe.

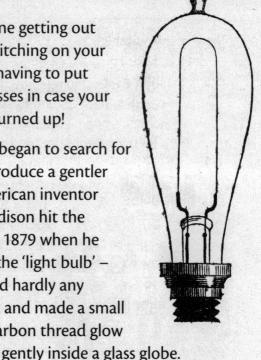

Now that the light bulb had been invented, people didn't just have access to cheap and easy lighting in their homes – they could stay up all night amusing one another with light-bulb jokes!

How many witches does it take to change a light bulb?

What do you want it changed into?

How many tourists does it take to change a light bulb?

Six. One to hold the bulb and five to ask for directions.

How many film stars does it take to change a light bulb?

One, but he only takes one step up the ladder, and then his stunt double takes over.

THOMAS EDISON
THE BUSY INVENTOR

The success of the light bulb made Edison rich and famous, and in 1889 he founded the 'Edison General Electric' company, which produced lots of other whizz-bang electrical devices.

He also designed the power stations, wiring, fuses, switches and sockets needed to get electricity into people's homes.

He also helped to build the first electric chair!

Thomas Edison

Not all his inventions caught on. He tried making furniture out of concrete, but it was too expensive (and hard!). He lost all the money he made from his electric inventions while trying to extract iron from rocks. But he had more hits than misses – he registered over 1,000 inventions with the Patent Office. Not bad for a man who was pretty useless at school!

His most successful and well-known inventions include a sound-recording machine called the phonograph.

He also made an early film camera, the kinetoscope, and projectors to show his films. But his most profitable invention was . . . an efficient battery.

Electricity helped solve another problem – how to get messages to people quickly.

'T-MAIL'

Even after the invention of steam trains and steam ships, sending messages over long distances still took quite a long time. You couldn't just send someone an e-mail or a text, you had to sit down and write a letter using a pen and paper. It took ages and the ink got everywhere! Then you had to take your letter to the post office and wait weeks or even months for it to arrive.

But once people knew how to use electricity, they were able to come up with a new invention that solved the problem of slow messages – the telegraph. Electrical signals were sent down wires that were laid along the side of railway tracks. Messages could now be sent and received in the blink of an eye!

An early telegraph office

MORSE CODE

In 1836, Samuel Morse developed a way to send messages through the telegraph – the electric current caused a metal point to push down on a strip of paper. When the current stopped, the metal point lifted off. If it just pressed down quickly it made a 'dot', if it stayed down longer it made a 'dash'. Different combinations of dots and dashes represented different letters and numbers. This way of sending messages became known as 'Morse code'.

A Morse telegraph machine

Mind you, it took a while for people to realize how useful this new invention was. For ten years the only people who sent telegrams were train operators, who used them to tell stationmasters what time the next train was coming in. But in 1844 two pickpockets escaped from London on a train bound for Slough. The police telegraphed Slough station, and as soon as the thieves got off the train, they were arrested.

Suddenly everyone wanted to send telegrams!

BAR CODES

Those strange sets of black and white lines that you find on the back of every item in the supermarket are called bar codes.

These codes contain tons of really handy information – for example a bar code on a packet of fish fingers tells you what they are, who made them, how much they cost, and how many are in stock.

When scanned with a laser, all this information can be recorded in a second. This is really useful when you've got hundreds of thousands of items going in and out of your store every day and you need to keep track of them all!

Bar codes were invented in 1949 by a whizz-kid American student called Norman Woodland and his buddy Bernard Silver.

The idea came to Norman as he was sitting on the beach in Florida. He was thinking about how information could be read by a laser. He remembered Morse code and how it was used to send information in dots and dashes.

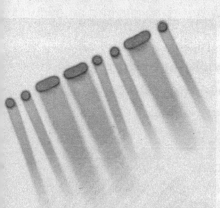

He drew dots and dashes in the sand, then pulled them down to form thin lines and thick lines – and bingo! His idea for a bar code was born!

Bar codes aren't just found on packets of fish fingers, they're used to track luggage in airports, shipping containers and nuclear waste. Researchers have even placed tiny bar codes on bees to study their mating habits!

THE FRISBEE

Baker William Russell Frisbie sold pies in metal pie-tins, which could be re-used or thrown away. One pie-eater threw his pie tin a little too hard, found it was aerodynamic and a new hit toy was born!

In 1948, Walter Frederick Morrison made a few changes, making one out of plastic and altering its shape to improve its speed and lift – he then sold it as the 'Frisbee'!

Did you know: In the 1960s the US Navy studied frisbees in wind tunnels with high-tech computers and built a special frisbee-launching machine to examine how they flew and try to use them in weapons launchers. They spent almost $400,000!

I'd have done it for a packet of dog biscuits!

THE DEATH RAY THAT NEVER WAS

One military invention that worked really well was created 25 years earlier, in the Second World War. Rumours had been going round that the Nazis had created a 'Death Ray' which used invisible radio waves to bring down British planes! This sent the Government into a panic, and a science boffin called Robert Watson-Watt was asked to make a British Death Ray.

After lots of experimenting, he decided it was impossible (it later turned out the Germans never made one either), but instead he came up with something else; a plane-detection system that used radio waves to spot planes coming even if they were a couple of hundred miles away.

Did he call it 'The Watson-Watt Plane-Detection System'?

Or 'The Magic Eye'?

It may not have been a 'Death Ray' but it was
a life saver for the British Air Force.

Or 'The-Machine-For-Spotting-Enemy-Planes-From-A-Long-Way-Away'?

No, he called it 'radar' . . .

Everyone knows that!

THE MICROWAVE

One young scientist in America was working on radar in the 1940s when he accidentally came up with another invention – the microwave oven!

Percy Spencer was developing a 'magnetron' – a special kind of tube that could produce beams of energy called 'microwaves'. One day he noticed that after standing next to the magnetron, the chocolate bar in his pocket had melted.

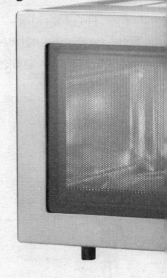

Instead of chucking it in the bin, Percy had an idea. Maybe his magnetron could be used to cook food? He put some popcorn kernels near the tube and within minutes he'd made popcorn!

Next he tried an egg, which exploded (as eggs do if you put them in microwaves).

He went on to help make the first microwave oven! You'd have had trouble fitting it into your kitchen – it was nearly two metres tall and weighed more than 300 kilograms!

Blimey, that's big – imagine how much popcorn you could make!

TOP TWENTY DAFT INVENTIONS

The famous scientist Albert Einstein once said, 'If at first an idea is not absurd, then there is no hope for it' . . . but some ideas are more absurd than others. Here are my favourite top twenty daft inventions!

1. THE AMPHIBIOUS BICYCLE – Sounds great, looks ridiculous. A bicycle that can be ridden on water! It was designed by a French inventor in the 1930s, and instead of wheels there were six large flotation balls, which rotated when you peddled. One puncture and you'd sink without trace.

Amphibian Bicycle Can Travel on Land or Water

The amphibian bicycle, left, ridden by its French inventor, has its supporting outrigger globes raised so it can be used for land travel

Drawing below, suggests the manner in which the bicycle, pictured at left, would drop the outrigger floats and be supported by them and the wheels in water travel

A HYBRID among vehicles, an amphibian bicycle that can travel on land or water, was demonstrated by its French inventor at a recent Paris exposition. Its wheels are hollow, bulbous floats that, with the aid of four smaller globes on outriggers, sus-

Inventor Hoeflich demonstrates his helmet-with-a-radio-inside (left). Tubes, antenna, and volume control are on top. At right, he lifts the lining to show the remainder of the radio circuit.

2. THE RADIO HAT –

The 'Man-from-Mars Radio Hat' went on sale in America in 1949. It was a helmet with a portable radio, which made it look a bit like your brain was plugged into some kind of mind-reading machine. It could pick up radio stations twenty miles away and came in colours such as flamingo pink, tangerine orange and lipstick red! The very first iPod!

You're not going out without your neck brush!

3. THE NECK BRUSH – This torture-like device was developed by a brush company in American in 1950, after a mother said she had trouble keeping her kid's neck clean. It's a large plastic collar with a brush inside which clamped around the neck and stopped it getting dirty. Imagine having to wear one of these all day!

4. UNDER-THE-BEDCLOTHES READING GLASSES – These were designed in the 1930s for people without bedside lamps, torches or common sense. They were a pair of reading glasses with tiny lights on top. They came with a long cord to plug into the large battery needed to power the lights!

5. THE EYE MASSAGER – If reading all those books under the bedclothes strained your eyes, you might want to try the multi-purpose eye massager. Place the rubber cups against your eye, and squeeze the bulbs to 'massage' your eyes by pushing in your eyeballs and twisting your eyelids. Ouch!

6. THE SELF-CLEANING HOUSE – Housewife Frances Gabe hated housework so much she designed a self-cleaning house! Each room had a box in the centre of the ceiling which sprayed soapy water everywhere, then gave it a good rinse and blow-dry! The furniture was waterproof, the floors sloped so that water could run off and any delicate objects were protected under glass.

7. THE PET UMBRELLA – A recent invention designed to keep your favourite pooch nice and dry while out for a walk in the rain.

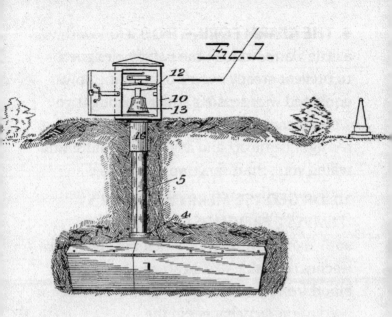

8. THE SAFETY COFFIN – A way to avoid the awkward and embarrassing moment when you find you have been accidentally buried alive. Before you were buried, strings were attached to your hands, head and feet and these were connected to a series of bells. If you woke up, you simply wiggled your hands and feet and alerted passers by. It came with a handy tube so that air could be pumped in until you could be dug up again.

9. THE ALARM FORK – This is a fork with a little alarm fitted in the handle, designed to prevent greedy people over-eating. It was equipped with sensors, and if it thought you were shoving too much cake into your face, a red light came on, and an alarm would sound telling you to put down your pudding!

10. DR GEORGE MERRYWEATHER'S 'TEMPEST PROGNOSTICATOR' – The aptly named Dr Merryweather believed that leeches (tiny slug-like creatures that suck blood from animals and humans) could be used to predict changes in the weather. He designed a machine made up of twelve glass bottles each containing a leech, which were connected to a small bell using various wires, chains and bits of whalebone. When the leeches sensed a change in the atmosphere they were supposed to climb up their bottles and trigger the bell.

11. THE RUSTLESS RAZOR – Inventor John Logie Baird was famous for inventing the television, but he had a few less successful ideas along the way. One was a shaving razor made with glass blades that never rusted. Unfortunately when he tried it on himself, the glass blades cut his face to shreds.

12. BALLOON SHOES – This was another mad invention by John Logie Baird – shoes with balloons in the soles, so you could walk more comfortably. When he tried them out, he found walking on balloons was tricky and passers-by thought he was drunk! Then one of the balloons popped and he fell over.

13. THE BABY CAGE – This was developed in the 1930s for people who lived in high-rise flats and wanted to give their darlings some fresh air and sunshine by putting them in a cage and hanging them out of the window! Really lucky children got one with a roof to keep out the rain, snow and bird poo.

14. CLAPPER MITTENS – Not getting enough applause in your life? Try James Crawford's 'Clapper Mittens'. These were basically two lumps of wood strapped to your hands, which you banged together to make a loud noise. Issue a pair to all your friends and get them to whack them whenever you walk past!

15. THE SNAKE WALKER – A snake lead for snake owners who want to take their scaly pet for a walk without it escaping and scaring the neighbours.

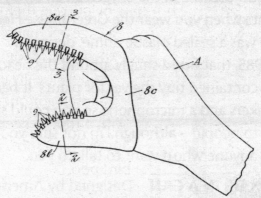

16. THE GUMS GLOVE – Designed in the 1930s, to save people from having to chew their food with their actual teeth. This was a glove with its own rubber teeth, which you could use to chomp your food for you.

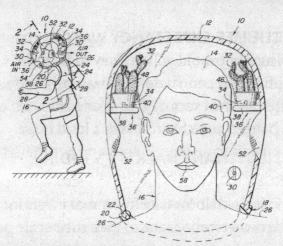

17. THE GREENHOUSE HELMET – Short of breath? Breathe in the oxygen given off by plants when you wear the Greenhouse Helmet! This was a sealed plastic dome, designed in 1985, that fitted snugly around the head and contained tiny shelves for plants. It had speakers and a microphone so you could still talk to people – although I'm not sure you'd find anyone who'd want to talk to you.

18. HAIR IN A CAN – Designed by American inventor Ron Popeil in the 1990s for men with bald spots. It was a fine powder to cover your dad's baldness, but looked about as realistic as if he'd gone to the local hardware shop and bought a can of brown spray paint to spray on his head!

19. THE LIFE-EXPECTANCY WATCH – It works out how old you're likely to be when you die, then counts down how long you've got left to the exact day, hour and minute. That'll keep you cheerful, won't it?

20. LIEUTENANT HALKETT'S INDIA-RUBBER BOAT CLOAK – The Victorians came up with lots of useful rubber inventions like bicycle tyres, mackintoshes, rubber bands and wellington boots, as well as some not-so-useful ones . . . like an inflatable boat cloak – a rubber cloak that could be pumped up with bellows stored in one pocket, and steered with paddles stored in the other!

QUIZ

Can you match these famous inventors to their most famous invention? Some of them are in this book, the rest are on my website: www.weirdworldofwonders.com

John Logie Baird

Alexander Graham Bell

Karl Benz

Laszlo Biro

Thomas Edison

Albert Einstein

Charles Goodyear

Johannes Gutenberg

Wilhelm Röntgen

Richard Trevithick

Robert Watson-Watt

Wilbur and Orville Wright

Ballpoint pen

Steam train

Internal combustion engine

Rubber tyres

Light bulb

Theory of relativity

Aeroplane

Television

Radar

Telephone

X-rays

Printing press

Also available in this series

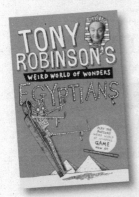
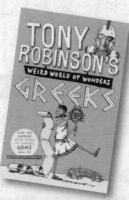
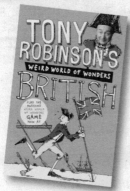
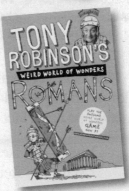

TONY ROBINSON'S
WEIRD WORLD OF WONDERS
WORLD WAR II

HELLO! JOIN ME AND THE CURIOSITY CREW AS WE
GALLOP HEADLONG THROUGH TIME, POINTING OUT
ALL THE MOST IMPORTANT, FUNNY, STRANGE,
AMAZING, SMELLY AND DISGUSTING BITS!
IT'S HISTORY, BUT NOT AS WE KNOW IT!

Find out everything you ever needed to
know about World War II in this brilliant,
action-packed, fact-filled book, including:

- Just how useful mashed potato is
- Why children were evacuated
- What it takes to be a spy
- How D-Day was kept a surprise

Win!

£100 of BOOKS
each for *you* and *your school!*

All you have to do is answer one VERY important question.

Imagine you're travelling to a *far away planet*, or a *desert island*, or even a *desert* . . . and, wherever you're going, there are **NO BOOKS**. Luckily, you're allowed to take just **ONE** book with you on your journey. What would it be?

For your chance to **WIN**, just tell us the name of your chosen book!

To enter go to **www.worldbookday.com**

BOOKs rock!

Want to read more?

VISIT your local bookshop

- Get great recommendations for books you'll love
- Meet your favourite authors & illustrators at brilliant events
- Discover books you never knew existed!

FIND YOUR LOCAL BOOKSHOP

www.booksellers.org.uk/bookshopsearch

JOIN your local library

You can browse and borrow from a huge selection of books and get recommendations of what to read next from expert librarians – all for FREE!

You can also discover libraries' wonderful children's and family reading activities – such as reading groups (*see* www.chatterbooks.org.uk), author events and challenges (*see* www.summerreadingchallenge.org.uk).

Get Online

Explore www.worldbookday.com to discover a world of bonkersly brilliant beautiful books!

- Downloads and activities for your favourite books and authors
- Cool games, trailers and videos
- Fantastic competitions
- Author events in your area
- Sign up for the **FREE** monthly e-newsletter

And much, much more...